Apple Pie Cookbook

*70+ Simple & Tasty Homemade Apple Pie
Recipes for the Whole Family
Delicious Apple Desserts Cookbook*

By Brendan Fawn

Introduction

Nowadays apples are the most popular fruits in America, but the first settlers from Europe were the ones who brought the apples and apple seeds to America. They also brought thousands of different baking apple recipes with them. Those apple dessert recipes were brought to America by waves of immigrants from different European countries – the Charlottes, Apple Strudels, Apfel Maultaschens from Germany, Switzerland, and Austria, Torta di Mele from Italy, Gâteau aux Pommes and Tartes from France, Dutch apple pies from Denmark, Sharlotka from Russia, Crumbles from England and many others.

The idiom *"as American as apple pie"* has a meaning of something very close and familiar to almost every American. Apple pie is the dessert that was brought by new settlers from various cultures, but in America, it became very popular and received nationwide love and affection and is still very popular.

In this cookbook, you will find various apple pies, cakes, charlottes, tortes, mini cakes, and other recipes. Everyone will find something tasty for himself.

Moreover, you don't need to be a professional 28 Michelin Star chef to use apple pie recipes from this cookbook and to prepare tasty apple desserts for yourself or your family. I would like to encourage you to test these apple pie recipes and to experiment with the ingredients adding your own flavors!

Apples – Magic Fruits

Apples are the most popular fruits among all the fruits of the world after mangoes and bananas.

"Even if you eat an apple a day, it will take you more than twenty years to try each of more than seven thousand varieties of apples grown all over the world".

Nowadays apples represent a kind of cultural icon in the Western world, despite the fact that they came from Asia, but actually, nobody knows for sure what their origin is. Despite that apples are legendary and very old fruits; people in ancient Greece already cultivated apple trees and had various kinds of apples. Almost all known nations and cultures of the ancient world have apples in their legends, myths, arts, and even religions. Apples appear almost in every widely known religious tradition as a symbol of wisdom, immortality and of course sin. Like the Christians, who have Adam and Eve and "apple of temptation", when it comes to the Bible where apple symbolizes temptation and sin. On the other hand, the ancient Greeks and their mythology used apples as a source and symbol of vitality and youth with their "golden apples of eternal youth" - the eleventh feat of Hercules.

Don't forget about the famous "golden apple of discord" from the ancient Greek mythology that was the main reason for the so-called Trojan War. In Scandinavian mythology, apples give eternal youth and Celtic symbolism considers the apple flower a symbol of fertility. It was about them, the apples, as the fruits of love that King Solomon mentioned: "..... refresh me with apples, for I am weary of love."

During the coronations of European Middle Ages and later ages monarchs, they were given the so-called "Imperial Apple", as the main attribute of power and leadership in Middle Ages societies and the symbol of law and king power.

"Present for more than thousand years in human history, apples became an important part of it as well as the part of world heritage and culture."

The famous legend of folk hero Wilhelm Telle from Switzerland, who had to shoot a bow at an apple on his son's head, is also widely known. We all know the story of Isaac Newton, who discovered the law of gravity and later created the theory of gravity when he was sitting under the apple tree and the apple fell from a tree on his head.

What about the vegetables? Well, some of the veggies have their names originated from apples. For example, did you know that our beloved tomato got its name from the Italian words that mean "golden apple". In the 18th century Russia, Catherine the Great, the Empress, ordered to breed "earth apples" or potatoes which caused major discontent of masses.

"The apple has around 20-30% of the air in it, which is why it does not sink in the water, so to get an apple out of the water, you don't need to dive".

Nowadays famous pop stars and bands are using the symbol of apple in their works - the legendary rock band The Beatles have used the apple in its Apple Corps logo.

Apples in the American Culture

Today the USA is among the biggest apples producing and exporting countries. Half the harvest of all fruit trees in the world is apples and they are mainly grown in four countries: in the USA, China, Turkey, and Poland. Maybe that is the reason why in modern American culture apples gained such big popularity. New York has been called the Big Apple and nowadays the apple name and symbol is used by one of the most successful computer companies in the world. What is more one of their products received the name of the most popular apple varieties in the USA – MacIntosh Red apples.

"We can say with confidence that by the time of the discovery of America by Columbus there were already thousands of sorts of apples in the world".

The apples themselves and apple seeds were first brought to America by migrants from northern Europe, mainly England and Holland at the beginning of the 17th century.

Apples saved people dozens of times during the human history and also in the United States in 1924 when the residents of Cornelia realized that apples saved their land from devastation and economy from complete collapse, so in honor of this event, they built a monument - a big red apple that you can visit in Cornelia, Georgia.

There is a well-known legend that even Thomas Jefferson, the author of the Declaration of Independence, who also was the president of the United States, supported the idea of cultivating apples. However, the most legendary folk hero in the field of the popularization of planting apple trees and apple orchards in the United States is undoubtedly Johnny Appleseed. For a long time, Apple Company has been using this folklore character in their iPhone as well as other device presentations and promotional materials.

Stories about Johnny Appleseed (John Chapman) say that he barefoot visited many American states and planted apple trees throughout the United States.

"By the way, the apples that Johnny Appleseed planted were not meant to be eaten, because they were tiny, hard and tasteless, however, they were perfect for ciders and other drinks".

For more than forty years, he crossed the country and popularized apples and planting them on all the free areas as well as taught settlers apple growing and cultivation.

American Apple Pie
- Symbol of USA

The first recipe for apple pie appeared in England and dates back to the beginning of the 14th century (about 1300-1320). Settlers from different European countries brought their own apple pies, cakes, tortes recipes as well as national habits and cultural elements and all this gave birth to the traditional American pie.

So the traditional American pie has the pastry laid on the bottom and side surfaces of a pie pan approximately 9 inches in diameter.

Then it is filled with the most important part of the apple pie which is, of course, a thick layer of apples, grated, sliced, cubed or cut into thin plates.

"Of the spices in the apple pie filling, the main are cinnamon, nutmeg, lemon juice, lime juice, orange juice, cloves, and some other spices".

The pastry apple pie cover is usually smooth and placed on top of the apple filling. At the same time, edges are gently pinned with the bottom pie layer at the upper border of the form. The traditional apple pie could also have a lattice top made of dough strips and could be served with cream, coffee, cocoa, strawberry or vanilla or another ice cream.

Gradually, the apple pie entered almost every American family and what is more became an important part of its life and today we can understand the young American boys who were far from home, on the battlefields of the Second World War, fighting in Europe, but who, when asked what it is worth fighting for, answered: "for mom and apple pie". Can we then doubt that apple pie became a real symbol of USA?

Grandma Apple Charlotte

*Prep Time: 10 min. | Baking Time: 55 min.
| Servings: 4*

Ingredients:

4 cups of sour and crisp Granny Smith apples, cubed
1 red apple (Red Delicious or McIntosh apple), sliced
1 cup of wheat flour
1 cup of sugar
4 eggs
2 tsp. baking powder
baking spray

How to Prepare:

1. Preheat the oven to 280°-300° Fahrenheit and then coat the pie pan with the baking spray.
2. Beat the eggs with the sugar using a hand mixer until the mixture becomes foamy and grows in volume at least two times.
3. Add the flour and beat the eggs mixture for 10 min. more. Then mix in the baking powder.

4. Spoon the cubed apples into the pie pan and slightly pour the eggs-flour mixture over the apples and then place the red apple slices on top.
5. Place the apple pie into the oven and bake it for 55 min. to serve with the cappuccino.

Nutritional Information:

Calories: 173; Total fat: 32 oz; Total carbohydrates: 35 oz; Protein: 19 oz

American Apple Pie

Prep Time: 20 min. | *Baking Time: 1 h*
| *Servings: 6*

Ingredients:
5 cups of wheat flour
1 tbsp. sunflower oil
5 tbsp. sugar
2 eggs
half cup of water
5 oz unsalted butter

Pie Filling:
8 apples, peeled and grated
4 tbsp. sugar
1 cup of wheat flour
1 tbsp. sunflower oil
4 tbsp. lime juice
Cinnamon and nutmeg

How to Prepare:

1. Preheat the oven to 280°-300° Fahrenheit and combine the wheat flour with the sugar. Then beat the eggs using a hand mixer and combine the eggs with the flour, water, butter and oil, mixing well.
2. Form the dough ball and then place it in the fridge for 4 hours.
3. Now let's prepare the pie filling - combine the grated apples with all the filling ingredients in a big bowl and mix well.
4. Half the dough ball and roll it out and then place one part of the dough into the pie pan 9" in diameter.
5. Place the pie filling on the dough and spread it with the spoon.
6. Add the second part of the dough on top and gently pin the edges with the bottom pie layer at the upper border of the pie pan and then place the sliced butter on top.
7. Bake the apple pie for 1 hour until the top of the pie is golden and crispy. Serve with the vanilla or chocolate ice cream.

Nutritional Information:

Calories: 131; Total fat: 18 oz; Total carbohydrates: 29 oz; Protein: 10 oz

Siberian Apple Torte

Prep Time: 15 min. | *Baking Time: 1 h*
| *Servings: 4*

Ingredients:
7 sour apples, grated
1 cup of wheat flour
1 cup of semolina
1 cup of sugar
2 tsp. baking soda
2 tbsp. cinnamon
5 oz unsalted butter, sliced

How to Prepare:
1. Preheat the oven to 280°-300° Fahrenheit and then coat the pie pan with the half of the butter and leave it in the oven to melt the butter.
2. Sprinkle grated apples with the cinnamon and leave for 10 min.
3. In a big kitchen bowl, combine the wheat flour, semolina, baking soda, and sugar and mix well.

4. Spoon 1/3 of the mixture into the pie pan and flatten with the spoon. Then place half of the apples and flatten with the spoon. Make two apples and three flour layers, remember that the flour mixture should be on top.
5. Place the sliced butter on top to cover the torte surface completely and bake the apple torte for 1 h to serve with the spray cream and coffee.

Nutritional Information:
Calories: 175; Total fat: 28 oz; Total carbohydrates: 37 oz; Protein: 19 oz

Grandma Mini Apple Pies

Prep Time: 5 min. | Baking Time: 30 min. | Servings: 5

Ingredients:
pie dough (could be frozen)
6 apples, peeled and sliced
1 cup of sugar
4 oz unsalted butter, sliced
2 tbsp. orange juice
2 tsp. cinnamon
2 oz peanuts

How to Prepare:

1. Preheat the oven to 250°-280° Fahrenheit.
2. Sprinkle the apples with the sugar and cinnamon and leave for 5 min.
3. Combine the apples with all the ingredients except for the pie dough and butter.

4. Coat the muffin pan with the butter, oil or cooking spray and then spread out the dough over the muffin pan. Cut out the dough with a glass or circular kitchen tool, but remember that the round crust should be bigger than a muffin.
5. Push down each round crust part into a muffin pan.
6. Spoon the apple filling into each pie crust and top with the butter.
7. Place the mini apple pies into the oven and bake for 30 min.!

Tips
You can use paper baking cups instead of the muffin pan.

Nutritional Information:
Calories: 140; Total fat: 16 oz; Total carbohydrates: 26 oz; Protein: 8 oz

Mini Muffin Apple Pies

Prep Time: 10 min. | *Baking Time: 1 h*
| *Servings: 10*

Ingredients:

pie crusts (could be frozen)
1 cup of wheat flour
1 tbsp. sunflower oil
4 tbsp. sugar
1 egg
5 tbsp. water
5 oz unsalted butter

Pie Filling:

6 apples, peeled and cubed
1 cup of sugar
2 tbsp. wheat flour
2 tbsp. lemon juice
2 tsp. cinnamon

How to Prepare:

1. Preheat the oven to 280°-300° Fahrenheit.
2. Combine the wheat flour with the sugar. Then add the eggs, water, and oil, beating well.
3. Form the dough ball and then place it in the fridge for 4 hours (Later we will cut it into strips).
4. Sprinkle the apples with the sugar and cinnamon and leave for 5 min. and then combine the apples with all the pie filling ingredients.
5. Coat the muffin pan with the butter, oil or cooking spray and then spread out the crust over the muffin pan. Cut out the crust with a glass or circular kitchen tool, but remember that the round crust should be bigger than a muffin.
6. Push down each round crust into muffin pans and then spoon the apple filling into pie crust.
7. Take the dough ball out of the fridge and roll out the dough and then cut it into thin strips.
8. Flatten the apple filling with a spoon and place the dough stripes on top.
9. Place the mini apple muffin pies into the oven and bake for 1 hour until the top of the pies has the golden brown color.

Nutritional Information:

Calories: 144; Total fat: 10 oz; Total carbohydrates: 18 oz; Protein: 9 oz

Mini Apple-Cherry Pies

Prep Time: 5 min. | *Baking Time: 1 h* | *Servings: 5*

Ingredients:

10 mini frozen pastry shells
7 apples, peeled and chopped
5 tbsp. cherry jam
4 tbsp. sugar
2 eggs
5 oz unsalted butter, sliced
2 tsp. cinnamon

How to Prepare:

1. Preheat the oven to 280°-300° Fahrenheit.
2. Let's prepare the pie filling: sprinkle the apples with the cinnamon and leave for 5 min. Wheat the eggs with the sugar using a hand mixer until they have a smooth and creamy consistency and then combine the apples with all the ingredients.
3. Place the apple-cherry filling into each pastry shell and flatten with the spoon.
4. Place the butter slices on each apple-cherry pie and then bake them for 1 hour until the top of the pies has a golden brown color.

Nutritional Information:

Calories: 145; Total fat: 11 oz; Total carbohydrates: 19 oz; Protein: 8 oz

Coconut Apple Pie

Prep Time: 5 min. | Baking Time: 40 min. | Servings: 2

Ingredients:

1 9" in diameter frozen pie crust (pastry shell)
5 apples, peeled and cubed
5 tbsp. shredded coconut
5 tbsp. coconut butter
4 tbsp. sugar
2 eggs
5 oz unsalted butter
2 tsp. cinnamon

How to Prepare:

1. Preheat the oven to 280°-300° Fahrenheit and melt the coconut butter in a pan.
2. Let's prepare the pie filling: sprinkle the apples with the cinnamon and leave for 5 min. Wheat the eggs with the sugar using a hand mixer until they have a

smooth and creamy consistency and then combine the apples with all the ingredients.

3. Place the apple-coconut filling into pastry shell and flatten with the spoon.
4. Place the coconut apple pie into the oven and bake for 40 min. until the top of the pies has a golden brown color.

Nutritional Information:

Calories: 145; Total fat: 11 oz; Total carbohydrates: 19 oz; Protein: 8 oz

Apple-Pineapple Pies

Prep Time: 5 min. | *Baking Time: 50 min.* | *Servings: 4*

Ingredients:
2 9" in diameter frozen pie crusts (pastry shells) or one square pastry shell
8 apples, peeled and cubed
8 oz round pineapple slices, canned
half cup of fresh or frozen raspberries
1 cup of brown sugar
2 eggs
2 tbsp. cream
5 oz unsalted butter
2 tsp. cinnamon

How to Prepare:

1. Preheat the oven to 280°-300° Fahrenheit.
2. Let's prepare the pie filling: sprinkle the apples with the cinnamon and leave for 5 min. Wheat the eggs with the sugar using a hand mixer until they have a

smooth and creamy consistency and then combine the apples with all the ingredients except for the pineapple slices.

3. Spoon the apple filling into two pastry shells or one square pastry shell and flatten with the spoon.

4. Place the round pineapple slices and raspberries on top and bake the apple-pineapple pie for 50 min. to serve with the cream on top.

Nutritional Information:

Calories: 157; Total fat: 18 oz; Total carbohydrates: 27 oz; Protein: 12 oz

Raspberries Apple Pie

Prep Time: 5 min. | *Baking Time: 40 min.*
| *Servings: 2*

Ingredients:

9" in diameter pie crust (pastry shell)
5 apples, peeled and grated
2 apples, sliced
1 cup of fresh raspberries
half cup of raspberry jam
half cup of sugar
5 tbsp. cream
5 oz unsalted butter

How to Prepare:

1. Preheat the oven to 280°-300° Fahrenheit and coat the muffin pan with the butter and then leave it in the oven to melt the butter.
2. Let's prepare the pie filling: sprinkle the 5 grated apples with the sugar. Combine the apples filling

with the raspberries jam, half of the fresh raspberries and cream and mix well using a spoon.

3. Place the apple filling into the pie crust and flatten with the spoon.
4. Add the sliced apples and fresh raspberries on top and bake the pie for 40 min. to serve with the cream on top.

Nutritional Information:

Calories: 156; Total fat: 18 oz; Total carbohydrates: 28 oz; Protein: 10 oz

Zurich Apple Pie

Prep Time: 5 min. | *Baking Time: 50 min.* | *Servings: 4*

Ingredients:

5 apples, peeled and cubed
1 cup of wheat flour
1 cup of sugar
3 eggs
1 tsp. baking powder
half tsp. salt
1 tsp. cinnamon
1 tsp. vanilla
half cup hazelnuts
3 oz unsalted butter

How to Prepare:

1. Preheat the oven to 280°-300° Fahrenheit and roast the hazelnuts for 5 min until golden brown. Then coat the pie pan with the butter and leave it in the oven to melt the butter.

2. Beat the eggs with the sugar using a hand mixer until the mixture becomes foamy and grows in volume at least two times.
3. Add the flour and beat the eggs mixture for 10 min. more. Then mix in the baking powder, salt, cinnamon, vanilla and stir in the roasted hazelnuts.
4. Place the cubed apples into the pie pan and slightly pour the flour and eggs mixture over the apples.
5. Place the apple pie into the oven and bake for 50 min. to serve with the berries jam.

Nutritional Information:

Calories: 161; Total fat: 19 oz; Total carbohydrates: 26 oz; Protein: 12 oz

Blueberries Apple Pie

Prep Time: 5 min. | **Baking Time: 1 h** | **Servings: 4**

Ingredients:
5 apples, peeled and chopped
1 cup blueberries fresh or frozen
1 cup of wheat flour
1 cup of sugar
3 eggs
1 tsp. baking powder
1 tsp. vanilla
3 oz unsalted butter

How to Prepare:

1. Preheat the oven to 150°-180° Fahrenheit and then coat the pie pan with the butter and leave it in the oven to melt the butter.
2. Beat the eggs with the sugar using a hand mixer until the mixture becomes foamy and grows in volume at least two times.

3. Add the flour and beat the eggs mixture for 10 min. more. Then mix in the baking powder, vanilla and stir in the blueberries.
4. Place the apples into the pie pan and slightly pour the blueberries and eggs mixture over the apples.
5. Place the apple pie into the oven and bake for 1 h to serve with the cream cheese, blueberries, strawberries, and raspberries.

Nutritional Information:

Calories: 164; Total fat: 23 oz; Total carbohydrates: 29 oz; Protein: 13 oz

Peanut Apple Pie

Prep Time: 5 min. | Baking Time: 50 min.
Servings: 4

Ingredients:
9" in diameter pie crust (pastry shell)
4 apples, peeled and grated
7 tbsp. peanut butter
half cup peanuts
half cup of wheat flour
half cup of sugar
2 tbsp. orange zest
1 tsp. baking powder
1 tsp. vanilla
3 oz unsalted butter

How to Prepare:

1. Preheat the oven to 200°-220° Fahrenheit and roast the peanuts and then coat the pie pan with the unsalted butter and leave it in the oven to melt the butter.

2. In a bowl, combine the flour, sugar, orange zest, baking powder, and vanilla and mix well. Stir in the peanuts and peanut butter and mix well until the mixture has a smooth consistency.
3. Place the apples into the pastry shell and spoon the peanuts filling on top and mix well.
4. Place the peanut apple pie into the oven and bake for 50 min.

Nutritional Information:

Calories: 177; Total fat: 24 oz; Total carbohydrates: 35 oz; Protein: 17 oz

Austrian Apple Pie

Prep Time: 5 min. | **Baking Time: 1 h** | **Servings: 4**

Ingredients:
1 cup of wheat flour
2 tsp. baking powder
1 tsp. vanilla
8 oz unsalted butter
baking spray

Filling:
8 apples, peeled and grated
1 cup of wheat flour
2 cups of sugar
1 tsp. cinnamon
5 tbsp. cream
half cup walnuts

How to Prepare:

1. Preheat the oven to 200°-220° Fahrenheit and roast the walnuts until golden brown and then coat the pie pan with the baking spray and leave it in the oven to melt the butter.
2. In a big bowl, combine the apples with 1 cup of the sugar and leave for 10 min.
3. In a second bowl, combine the flour, baking powder, butter, and vanilla and mix well.
4. Blend the mixture with the water until the dough has a smooth consistency and then pin out the dough and place it into the pie pan.
5. Let's prepare the pie filling now – combine the flour with the sugar, cinnamon, and walnuts.
6. Spoon half of the apples on the crust and then spoon half of the flour mixture on top. Top with the grated apples and the second part of the flour mixture. Pour the cream and place the butter slices on top.
7. Place the apple pie into the oven and bake for 1 hour until the top of the pie is golden brown and crispy.

Nutritional Information:

Calories: 187; Total fat: 25 oz; Total carbohydrates: 37 oz; Protein: 18 oz

Walnuts Apple Pie

Prep Time: 5 min. | *Baking Time: 50 min.*
Servings: 4

Ingredients:
9" in diameter pie crust (pastry shell)
5 apples, peeled and chopped
1 cup walnuts, ground
1 cup of sugar
half cup liquid honey
1 tbsp. lemon zest
1 tsp. baking powder
1 tsp. vanilla
5 oz unsalted butter

How to Prepare:

1. Preheat the oven to 150°-180° Fahrenheit and then coat the pie pan with the unsalted butter and leave it in the oven to melt the butter.
2. In a bowl, combine the sugar, lemon zest, baking powder, and vanilla and mix well.
3. Combine the walnuts with the liquid honey and mix and then spoon the honey mixture into the sugar mixture.
4. In a bowl, combine the apples with the honey-walnuts filling and mix well.
5. Spoon the walnuts apple filling into the pastry shell pie and bake in the oven for 50 min.

Nutritional Information:
Calories: 166; Total fat: 25 oz; Total carbohydrates: 37 oz; Protein: 15 oz

Peaches Apple Pie

Prep Time: 5 min. | Baking Time: 1 h | Servings: 4

Ingredients:
5 apples, peeled and chopped
1 can of canned peaches, sliced
1 cup of wheat flour
1 cup of sugar
3 eggs
1 tsp. baking powder
1 tsp. vanilla
5 oz unsalted butter

How to Prepare:
1. Preheat the oven to 150°-180° Fahrenheit and then coat the pie pan with the butter and leave it in the oven to melt the butter.
2. Beat the eggs with the sugar using a hand mixer until the mixture becomes foamy and grows in volume at least two times.
3. Add the flour and beat the eggs mixture for 10 min. more. Then mix in the baking powder and vanilla.
4. Place the sliced peaches into the pie pan and then place the apples on top. Slightly pour the eggs mixture over the apples.
5. Place the apple pie into the oven and bake it for 1 h to serve with the spray cream.

Nutritional Information:
Calories: 174; Total fat: 29 oz; Total carbohydrates: 37 oz; Protein: 17 oz

Apple Pie with Toffees

Prep Time: 5 min. | *Baking Time: 40 min.* |
Servings: 4

Ingredients:

9" in diameter pie crust (pastry shell)
one cup toffee bits, chopped
5 apples, peeled and grated
1 cup of brown sugar
5 tbsp. liquid honey
1 tsp. cinnamon
half tsp. cloves, ground
5 oz unsalted butter

How to Prepare:

1. In a saucepan, combine the apples, sugar, butter, cinnamon and cloves and stew for 20 min. over low heat with the closed lid until the smooth consistency. Pour the honey over the mixture when it is ready.
2. Spoon the mixture into the pastry shell and add half of the toffees on top, bake in the oven for 40 min.
3. 10 min. before the pie is ready, open the oven and sprinkle some toffee bits on top.

Nutritional Information:

Calories: 149; Total fat: 20 oz; Total carbohydrates: 32 oz; Protein: 12 oz

Winter Apple Pie

Prep Time: 5 min. | *Baking Time: 40 min.* |
Servings: 2

Ingredients:

9" in diameter pie crust (pastry shell)
4 apples, peeled and grated
7 tbsp. apple jam
1 cup of brown sugar
2 inch of ginger, minced
3 tsp. vanilla
half tsp. cloves, ground
5 oz unsalted butter

How to Prepare:

1. In a saucepan, combine the apples, apple jam, sugar, ginger, vanilla, butter and cloves and stew for 10 min. over medium heat, stirring all the time.
2. Spoon the mixture into the pastry shell and bake in the oven for 40 min. and serve with the hot Glühwein.

Nutritional Information:

Calories: 141; Total fat: 18 oz; Total carbohydrates: 30 oz; Protein: 10 oz

Pears Apple Pie

Prep Time: 5 min. | Baking Time: 40 min. |
Servings: 4

Ingredients:
5 apples, peeled and sliced
5 fresh pears, sliced
1 cup of wheat flour
1 cup of sugar
1 cup of oats
1 tsp. baking powder
1 cup of walnuts, ground
1 tsp. cinnamon
10 oz unsalted butter

How to Prepare:

1. Preheat the oven to 230°-260° Fahrenheit and then coat the pie pan with the butter and leave it in the oven to melt the butter.

2. Place the pears and half of the apples into a baking pan.
3. Melt the unsalted butter. In a bowl, combine all the ingredients except for the apples and pour the mixture over the pears and apples.
4. Place the sliced apples on top and bake for 40 min. until pears and apples are soft. Serve with the spray cream or vanilla ice cream.

Nutritional Information:

Calories: 168; Total fat: 28 oz; Total carbohydrates: 37 oz; Protein: 18 oz

Lemon Apple Pie

Prep Time: 5 min. | *Baking Time: 50 min.* |
Servings: 4

Ingredients:

9" in diameter pie crust (pastry shell)
1 lemon, sliced
4 tbsp. lemon zest
6-7 sweet Gala or Fuji apples, peeled and grated
1 cup of sugar
5 tbsp. liquid honey
1 tsp. cinnamon
half tsp. cloves, ground
5 oz unsalted butter

How to Prepare:

1. In a saucepan, combine the apples, sugar, butter, cinnamon, lemon zest and cloves and stew for 20 min. over low heat with the closed lid. Pour the honey over the mixture when it is ready.

2. Spoon the mixture into the pastry shell and place the sliced lemon on top, bake in the oven for 50 min.

Nutritional Information:

Calories: 147; Total fat: 22 oz; Total carbohydrates: 34 oz; Protein: 13 oz

Sour Apricots Apple Pie

Prep Time: 5 min. | **Baking Time: 1 h** | **Servings: 4**

Ingredients:

4 cups of sour Granny Smith apples, chopped
2 cups of dried apricots
1 cup of wheat flour
1 cup of sugar
3 eggs
1 tsp. baking powder
1 tsp. vanilla
5 oz unsalted butter

How to Prepare:

1. Soak the dried apricots in the warm water and then cube them.
2. Preheat the oven to 150°-180° Fahrenheit and then coat the pie pan with the butter and leave it in the oven to melt the butter.
3. Beat the eggs with the sugar using a hand mixer until the mixture becomes foamy and grows in volume at least two times.
4. Add the flour and beat the eggs mixture for 10 min. more. Then mix in the baking powder and vanilla. Stir in the cubed apricots.
5. Place the apples into the pie pan and slightly pour the eggs and apricots mixture over the apples.
6. Place the apple pie into the oven and bake it for 1 h to serve with the spray cream on top.

Nutritional Information:

Calories: 179; Total fat: 30 oz; Total carbohydrates: 35 oz; Protein: 18 oz

Raisins Apple Pie

Prep Time: 5 min. | **Baking Time: 1 h** | **Servings: 4**

Ingredients:

5 sweet Ambrosia apples, peeled and cubed
2 cups of raisins
1 cup of wheat flour
1 cup of sugar
3 eggs
1 tsp. baking powder
2 tbsp. orange zest
1 tsp. cinnamon
5 oz unsalted butter

How to Prepare:

1. Soak the raisins in the warm water for 20 min.
2. Preheat the oven to 150°-180° Fahrenheit and then coat the pie pan with the butter and leave it in the oven to melt the butter.

47

3. Beat the eggs with the sugar using a hand mixer until the mixture becomes foamy and grows in volume at least two times.
4. Add the flour and beat the eggs mixture for 10 min. more. Then mix in the baking powder, orange zest, and cinnamon and mix well. Stir in the raisins.
5. Place the apples into the pie pan and slightly pour the eggs and raisins mixture over the apples.
6. Place the apple pie into the oven and bake it for 1 hour to serve with the strawberry ice cream.

Nutritional Information:

Calories: 175; Total fat: 28 oz; Total carbohydrates: 38 oz; Protein: 16 oz

Chocolate Apple Pie

Prep Time: 5 min. | *Baking Time: 50 min.* |
Servings: 4

Ingredients:

5 apples, peeled and chopped
1 cup dark chocolate, cubed
1 cup of wheat flour
1 cup of sugar
3 eggs
1 tsp. baking powder
1 tsp. vanilla
3 oz unsalted butter

How to Prepare:

1. Preheat the oven to 150°-180° Fahrenheit and then coat the pie pan with the butter and leave it in the oven to melt the butter.
2. Beat the eggs with the sugar using a hand mixer until the mixture becomes foamy and grows in volume at least two times.
3. Add the flour and beat the eggs mixture for 10 min. more. Then mix in the baking powder, vanilla and stir in the chocolate cubes.
4. Place the apples into the pie pan and slightly pour the chocolate and eggs mixture over the apples.
5. Place the apple pie into the oven and bake for 50 min. to serve with the spray cream.

Nutritional Information:

Calories: 164; Total fat: 23 oz; Total carbohydrates: 34 oz; Protein: 13 oz

Birthday Choco Apple Pie

Prep Time: 5 min. | **Baking Time: 1 h** | **Servings: 4**

Ingredients:

7 apples, peeled and chopped
1 cup dark chocolate, cubed
8 tbsp. cocoa powder
1 cup of wheat flour
1 cup of sugar
3 eggs
1 tsp. baking powder
1 tsp. vanilla
3 oz unsalted butter

How to Prepare:

1. Preheat the oven to 150°-180° Fahrenheit and then coat the pie pan with the butter and leave it in the oven to melt the butter.

2. Beat the eggs with the sugar using a hand mixer until the mixture becomes foamy and grows in volume at least two times.
3. Add the flour with cocoa powder and beat the eggs mixture for 10 min. more. Then mix in the baking powder, vanilla and stir in the chocolate cubes.
4. Place the apples into the pie pan and slightly pour the chocolate and eggs mixture over the apples.
5. Place the apple pie into the oven and bake for 1 hour, then melt the dark chocolate on low heat for around 10 min., stirring all the time and after cooling pour it slowly over the apple pie to serve!

Nutritional Information:
Calories: 169; Total fat: 25 oz; Total carbohydrates: 39 oz; Protein: 17 oz

Lemon Coconut Apple Pie

Prep Time: 5 min. | Baking Time: 40 min.
Servings: 4

Ingredients:
9" in diameter pie crust (pastry shell)
5 apples, peeled and grated
6 tbsp. lemon zest, minced
8 oz coconut butter
3 tbsp. shredded coconut
1 cup of sugar
1 tsp. cinnamon
1 tsp. vanilla

How to Prepare:

1. In a saucepan, combine the apples, lemon zest, coconut butter, sugar, cinnamon, and vanilla and boil over low heat with the closed lid until the smooth consistency.

2. Spoon the mixture into the pastry shell and sprinkle the shredded coconut on top, bake in the oven for 40 min.

Nutritional Information:

Calories: 147; Total fat: 21 oz; Total carbohydrates: 33 oz; Protein: 13 oz

Mini Macadamia Apple Pies

Prep Time: 5 min. | **Baking Time: 1 h** | **Servings: 5**

Ingredients:

10 mini frozen pie crusts (pastry shells)
5 Cortland or Cameo apples, peeled and grated
1 cup of macadamia nuts, ground
5 tbsp. apple jam
5 tbsp. sugar
2 eggs
5 oz unsalted butter, sliced
2 tsp. cinnamon

How to Prepare:

1. Preheat the oven to 280°-300° Fahrenheit. Roast the macadamia nuts in the oven for 10 min. until lightly browned and crispy.
2. Grind the macadamia nuts using a blender or a food processor.
3. Let's prepare the pies filling: sprinkle the apples with the cinnamon and leave for 5 min. Wheat the eggs with the sugar using a hand mixer until it has a smooth and creamy consistency and then combine the apples with all the ingredients.
4. Place the pies filling into each pie crust and flatten with the spoon.
5. Place the butter slices on each macadamia pie and then bake them for 1 hour to serve with the spray cream on top.

Tips

If you like crispy and well-roasted nuts then you can toast the macadamia nuts in the oven for 20 min. until well browned.

Nutritional Information:

Calories: 147; Total fat: 12 oz; Total carbohydrates: 29 oz; Protein: 10 oz

Fast Coconut Apple Cake

Prep Time: 5 min. | *Baking Time: 40 min.*
Servings: 6

Ingredients:
1 package of French vanilla cake mix
5 sweet Golden Delicious apples, peeled and grated
5 tbsp. shredded coconut
3 tbsp. coconut butter
half cup sugar
5 oz unsalted butter, sliced
2 tsp. cinnamon

How to Prepare:

1. Preheat the oven to 150°-180° Fahrenheit and then coat the pie pan with the butter and leave it in the oven to melt the butter.
2. Follow the instructions suggested on the packet to prepare the French vanilla cake mix and combine the mix with the apples, coconut butter, sugar, and cinnamon.
3. Sprinkle the shredded coconut on top and bake the cake, following the instructions given.
4. Cool the apple cake and place it into the fridge for at least few hours and then serve with the spray cream.

Nutritional Information:
Calories: 139; Total fat: 15 oz; Total carbohydrates: 39 oz; Protein: 15 oz

Pumpkin Apple Pie

Prep Time: 5 min. | Baking Time: 50 min. |
Servings: 4

Ingredients:

2 sour apples, peeled and grated
6 oz pumpkin, peeled and grated
1 cup of wheat flour
1 cup of sugar
3 eggs
1 tsp. baking powder
1 tsp. vanilla
3 oz unsalted butter

How to Prepare:

1. Preheat the oven to 150°-180° Fahrenheit and then coat the silicone pie pan with the butter.
2. Beat the eggs with the sugar using a hand mixer until the mixture becomes foamy and grows in volume at least two times.

3. Add the flour and beat the eggs mixture for 10 min. more. Then mix in the baking powder, vanilla and mix in the apples and pumpkin.
4. Pour the mixture into the silicone pic pan and bake the pie for 50 min. to serve with the spray cream.

Nutritional Information:

Calories: 169; Total fat: 24 oz; Total carbohydrates: 38 oz; Protein: 14 oz

Almond Apple Pie

Prep Time: 5 min. | Baking Time: 50 min. | Servings: 4

Ingredients:

4 sweet apples, peeled and grated
3 sour apples, peeled and grated
2 tbsp. almonds
1 cup of almond flour
1 tsp. pure almond extract
1 cup of sugar
3 eggs
1 tsp. baking powder
1 tsp. vanilla
3 oz unsalted butter

How to Prepare:

1. Preheat the oven to 150°-180° Fahrenheit and then coat the silicone pie pan with the butter.

2. Beat the eggs with the sugar using a hand mixer until the mixture becomes foamy and grows in volume at least two times.
3. Spoon the almond flour and beat the eggs mixture for 10 min. more. Then mix in the baking powder, vanilla, almond extract and mix in the apples.
4. Pour the mixture into the silicone pie pan and place the almonds on top, then bake the pie for 50 min. to serve.

Nutritional Information:

Calories: 175; Total fat: 27 oz; Total carbohydrates: 39 oz; Protein: 15 oz

Zucchini Apple Pie

Prep Time: 5 min. | Baking Time: 50 min. |
Servings: 4

Ingredients:

5 apples, peeled and grated
1 small zucchini, peeled and grated
1 cup of wheat flour
1 cup of sugar
3 eggs
1 tsp. baking powder
half tsp. nutmeg
half tsp. salt
half cup walnuts
3 oz unsalted butter

How to Prepare:

1. Preheat the oven to 280°-300° Fahrenheit and roast the walnuts for 5 min until golden brown. Then coat the pie pan with the butter and leave it in the oven to melt the butter.
2. Beat the eggs with the sugar using a hand mixer until the mixture becomes foamy and grows in volume at least two times.
3. Add the flour and beat the eggs mixture for 10 min. more. Then mix in the baking powder, salt, nutmeg and stir in the zucchini and roasted walnuts.
4. Place the cubed apples into the pie pan and slightly pour the flour and eggs mixture over the apples.
5. Place the apple pie into the oven and bake for 50 min. to serve with the orange jam.

Nutritional Information:

Calories: 178; Total fat: 25 oz; Total carbohydrates: 36 oz; Protein: 14 oz

Caramel Apple Cake

Prep Time: 5 min. | Baking Time: 40 min.
Servings: 6

Ingredients:
5 sweet and crunchy Red Delicious apples, peeled and grated
1 package of Spice cake mix
2 cups of caramel sauce
3 tbsp. coconut butter
4 oz unsalted butter, sliced
2 tsp. cinnamon

How to Prepare:
1. Preheat the oven to 150°-180° Fahrenheit and then coat the silicone pie pan with the butter and leave it in the oven to melt the butter.
2. Follow the instructions suggested on the packet to prepare the Spice cake mix and combine the mix with the apples, coconut butter, and cinnamon.

Then stir in the half of the caramel sauce and mix well until the homogenous mass.

3. Bake the cake, following the instructions given and then cool the cake for few hours and pour remaining caramel over the cake to serve with the chocolate ice cream.

Nutritional Information:

Calories: 140; Total fat: 16 oz; Total carbohydrates: 32 oz; Protein: 14 oz

Carrots Apple Cake

Prep Time: 5 min. | Baking Time: 40 min. |
Servings: 6

Ingredients:

5 sweet apples, peeled and grated
1 package of Carrot cake mix
1 cup of carrots, grated
half cup of wheat flour
half cup of cream
4 oz unsalted butter, sliced
2 tsp. cinnamon
1 tsp. nutmeg

How to Prepare:

1. Preheat the oven to 150°-180° Fahrenheit and then coat the silicone pie pan with the butter and leave it in the oven to melt the butter.
2. Follow the instructions suggested on the packet to prepare the Carrot cake mix and combine the mix

with the apples, nutmeg, flour, cream, and cinnamon. Then stir in the grated carrots and mix well until the homogenous mass.

3. Bake the cake, following the instructions given and cool the cake for few hours and then serve with the spray cream on top.

Nutritional Information:

Calories: 162; Total fat: 27 oz; Total carbohydrates: 38 oz; Protein: 19 oz

Carrots and Walnuts Apple Pie

Prep Time: 5 min. | *Baking Time: 40 min.* |
Servings: 6

Ingredients:

5 sweet apples, peeled and grated
1 cup of carrots, grated
1 cup of walnuts
3 eggs
7 tbsp. sunflower oil
1 cup of sugar
1 cup wheat flour
1 tbsp. baking powder
1 oz unsalted butter, sliced
2 tsp. cinnamon
1 tsp. nutmeg

How to Prepare:

1. Preheat the oven to 280°-300° Fahrenheit and roast the walnuts for 5 min until golden brown. Then coat the non-stick pie pan with the butter and leave it in the oven to melt the butter.
2. Combine all the dry ingredients: sugar, wheat flour, baking powder, cinnamon, and nutmeg and mix well.
3. Then combine the apples with the carrots, oil, and eggs and beat well.
4. Spoon the dry ingredients into the mix and stir in the walnuts, then mix well.
5. Pour the apple dough into the non-stick pie pan and bake for 50 min.

Nutritional Information:

Calories: 145; Total fat: 21 oz; Total carbohydrates: 36 oz; Protein: 15 oz

Sweet Peanut Apple Cake

Prep Time: 10 min. | Baking Time: 55 min.
Servings: 6

Ingredients:
2 cups sweet apple jam
1 cup peanut butter
1 cup of sugar
2 eggs
1 cup wheat flour
1 tsp. baking soda
half tsp. salt
4 oz unsalted butter, sliced
2 tsp. cinnamon
baking spray

How to Prepare:

1. Preheat the oven to 150°-180° Fahrenheit and then coat the pie pan with the baking spray.

2. Combine all the dry ingredients: sugar, wheat flour, baking soda, butter, salt, and cinnamon.
3. Combine the peanut butter and butter and mix well. Then stir in the eggs and apple jam and mix well until the homogenous mass.
4. Finally, combine all the ingredients and pour into the pie pan and bake the cake for 55 min. to serve.

Nutritional Information:

Calories: 145; Total fat: 20 oz; Total carbohydrates: 34 oz; Protein: 15 oz

German Chocolate Apple Cake

Prep Time: 5 min. | **Baking Time: 40 min.** | **Servings: 6**

Ingredients:

5 sour apples, peeled and grated
1 package of German chocolate cake mix
1 cup of raisins
4 oz unsalted butter, sliced
2 tsp. cinnamon
1 tsp. nutmeg

How to Prepare:

1. Soak the raisins in the warm water for 20 min. and then preheat the oven to 280°-300° Fahrenheit.
2. Follow the instructions suggested on the packet to prepare the German chocolate cake mix and combine the mix with the apples, nutmeg, and cinnamon. Then stir in the raisins and mix well until the homogenous mass.
3. Bake the cake, following the instructions given and cool it for few hours and then serve with the spray cream.

Nutritional Information:

Calories: 155; Total fat: 25 oz; Total carbohydrates: 39 oz; Protein: 17 oz

Choco Apple Cake

Prep Time: 5 min. | *Baking Time: 40 min.*
Servings: 6

Ingredients:

2 apples, peeled and chopped
1 cup of cocoa powder
1 cup of sugar
1 cup cream
2 eggs
1 cup wheat flour
1 tsp. baking powder
half tsp. salt
7 oz unsalted butter, sliced
2 tsp. cinnamon
1 tsp. nutmeg

How to Prepare:

1. In a bowl combine all the dry ingredients: cocoa powder, sugar, flour, salt, cinnamon, and nutmeg.
2. Melt the butter in a pan and mix in the sugar. Then add the eggs and cream, stir well. Mix in the dry ingredients and stir until the smooth consistency.
3. Then add in the apples, mix well and preheat the oven to 290°-310° Fahrenheit to bake the cake for 40 min.

Nutritional Information:

Calories: 148; Total fat: 24 oz; Total carbohydrates: 37 oz; Protein: 16 oz

Coffee Apple Cake

Ingredients:

2 apples, peeled and chopped
2 tbsp. pure coffee extract
1 tbsp. espresso powder
1 cup of sugar
1 cup heavy cream
2 eggs
1 cup wheat flour
1 tsp. baking powder
half tsp. salt
7 oz unsalted butter, sliced
2 tsp. cinnamon
1 tsp. nutmeg

How to Prepare:

1. In a bowl combine all the dry ingredients: pure coffee extract, espresso powder, sugar, flour, salt, cinnamon, and nutmeg.
2. Melt the butter in a pan and mix in the sugar. Then add the eggs and heavy cream, stir well. Mix in the dry ingredients and stir until the smooth consistency.
3. Then add in the apples and mix well, preheat the oven to 290°-310° Fahrenheit and bake the cake for 50 min.

Nutritional Information:

Calories: 150; Total fat: 25 oz; Total carbohydrates: 36 oz; Protein: 17 oz

Banana Apple Pie

Prep Time: 5 min. | Baking Time: 50 min. |
Servings: 4

Ingredients:

4 sweet apples, peeled and grated
3 bananas, cubed
1 tsp. pure banana extract
1 cup of wheat flour
1 cup of sugar
3 eggs
1 tsp. baking powder
1 tsp. vanilla
3 oz unsalted butter

How to Prepare:

1. Preheat the oven to 150°-180° Fahrenheit and then coat the silicone pie pan with the butter.
2. Beat the eggs with the sugar using a hand mixer until the mixture becomes foamy and grows in volume at least two times.
3. Add the flour and beat the eggs mixture for 10 min. more. Then mix in the baking powder, vanilla, pure banana extract and mix in the apples and cubed bananas.
4. Pour the mixture into the silicone pie pan and bake the pie for 50 min. to serve with the banana ice cream.

Nutritional Information:

Calories: 168; Total fat: 26 oz; Total carbohydrates: 31 oz; Protein: 15 oz

Strawberry Apple Cake

Prep Time: 5 min. | *Baking Time: 50 min.* |
Servings: 6

Ingredients:
1 package of Strawberry cake mix
frozen dough strips
5 apples, peeled and grated
5 tbsp. strawberry jam
4 tbsp. cherry jam
half cup sugar
5 oz unsalted butter, sliced
2 tsp. vanilla

How to Prepare:

1. Preheat the oven to 150°-180° Fahrenheit and then coat the pie pan with the butter and leave it in the oven to melt the butter.
2. Follow the instructions suggested on the packet to prepare the Strawberry cake mix and combine the

mix with the apples, strawberry jam, sugar, and vanilla.

3. Spoon the cherry jam and place the crust strips on top to bake the cake, following the instructions given.

4. Cool the apple cake and place it into the fridge for at least few hours and then serve with the vanilla ice cream and cappuccino.

Nutritional Information:

Calories: 168; Total fat: 24 oz; Total carbohydrates: 38 oz; Protein: 12 oz

Macadamia Apple Pie

Ingredients:

9" in diameter pie crust (pastry shell)
5 apples, peeled and chopped
half cup macadamia nuts, chopped
3 eggs
half cup of milk
half cup of cream cheese
1 cup of sugar
1 tsp. baking powder
1 tsp. vanilla
3 oz unsalted butter

How to Prepare:

1. Preheat the oven to 200°-220° Fahrenheit and roast the macadamia nuts and then coat the pie pan with the unsalted butter and place the pastry shell inside.
2. In a bowl, combine the apples, half of the sugar, baking powder and vanilla and mix well. Stir in the macadamia nuts and spoon the mixture into the pastry shell.
3. Bake the pie for 20 min. and then cool the apple pie, but don't remove from the pie pan.
4. Beat the remaining sugar with the cream cheese until the smooth consistency and then add the milk, eggs and pour some water. Now whisk the mixture until it has a homogenous mass and smooth consistency, use a hand mixer.
5. When the mixture is ready, spoon it over the apple pie and bake for 35 min. until the light brown color.

Nutritional Information:

Calories: 200; Total fat: 44 oz; Total carbohydrates: 55 oz; Protein: 27 oz

Two-Layer Coconut Apple Pie

Prep Time: 10 min. | **Baking Time: 50 min.** |
Servings: 4

Ingredients:

9" in diameter pie crust (pastry shell)
5 apples, peeled and chopped
8 tbsp. shredded coconut
2 eggs
half cup of coconut milk
half cup of cream cheese
1 cup of sugar
1 tsp. baking powder
1 tsp. vanilla
3 oz unsalted butter

How to Prepare:

1. Preheat the oven to 200°-220° Fahrenheit and then coat the pie pan with the unsalted butter and place the pastry shell inside.
2. In a bowl, combine the apples, half of the sugar, baking powder and vanilla and mix well. Stir in the shredded coconut and spoon the mixture into the pastry shell.
3. Bake the pie for 20 min. and then cool the apple pie, but don't remove from the pie pan.
4. Beat the remaining sugar with the cream cheese until the smooth consistency and then add the coconut milk, eggs and pour some water. Now whisk the mixture until it has a homogenous mass and smooth consistency, use a hand mixer.
5. When the mixture is ready, spoon it over the apple pie and bake the pie for 30 min. more.
6. 5 min. before the pie is ready open the oven and sprinkle some shredded coconut over the apple pie.

Nutritional Information:

Calories: 198; Total fat: 42 oz; Total carbohydrates: 52 oz; Protein: 24 oz

Two-Layer Strawberry Apple Pie

Prep Time: 5 min. | ***Baking Time: 50 min.*** |
Servings: 4

Ingredients:
9" in diameter pie crust (pastry shell)
5 apples, peeled and chopped
5 big fresh strawberries, sliced
half cup of strawberry jam
2 eggs
half cup of milk
half cup of cream cheese
1 cup of sugar
1 tsp. vanilla
3 oz unsalted butter

How to Prepare:

1. Preheat the oven to 200°-220° Fahrenheit and then coat the pie pan with the unsalted butter and place the pastry shell inside.
2. In a bowl, combine the apples, half of sugar and vanilla and mix well to spoon the mixture into the pastry shell.
3. Bake the pie for 10 min. and then cool the apple pie, but don't remove from the pie pan.
4. Spoon the strawberry jam over the apple pie and then place the sliced strawberries on top.
5. Beat the remaining sugar with the cream cheese until the smooth consistency and then stir in the milk and eggs. Now whisk the mixture until it has a homogenous mass and smooth consistency, use a hand mixer.

6. When the mixture is ready spoon it over the apples and strawberry pie and bake for 50 min. to serve with the vanilla ice cream.

Nutritional Information:

Calories: 197; Total fat: 41 oz; Total carbohydrates: 52 oz; Protein: 25 oz

Two-Layer Pineapple Apple Pie

Prep Time: 5 min. | **Baking Time: 50 min.**
Servings: 4

Ingredients:

9" in diameter pie crust (pastry shell)
5 apples, peeled and chopped
8 oz round pineapple slices, canned
2 tbsp. pure pineapple extract
2 eggs
half cup of milk
half cup of cream cheese
1 cup of sugar
1 tsp. cinnamon
3 oz unsalted butter
baking spray

How to Prepare:

1. Preheat the oven to 200°-220° Fahrenheit and then coat the pie pan with the unsalted butter or baking spray and place the pastry shell inside.
2. In a bowl, combine the apples, half of the sugar, pineapple extract and cinnamon and mix well to spoon the mixture into the pastry shell.
3. Bake the pie for 10 min. and then cool the apple pie and place the pineapple slices over the apple pie.
4. Beat the remaining sugar with the cream cheese until the smooth consistency and then stir in the milk, butter, and eggs. Now whisk the mixture until it has a homogenous mass and smooth consistency, use a hand mixer.
5. When the mixture is ready spoon it over the apples and pineapples and bake for 50 min. to serve with the spray cream.

Nutritional Information:

Calories: 194; Total fat: 39 oz; Total carbohydrates: 50 oz;
Protein: 22 oz

Forest Berries Apple Pie

Prep Time: 15 min. | *Baking Time: 1 h* |
Servings: 4

Ingredients:

9" in diameter pie crust (pastry shell)
5 apples, peeled and chopped
1 cup of blueberries
1 cup of cranberries
1 cup of sugar
5 tbsp. wheat flour
5 tbsp. of apple jam
5 tbsp. of hazelnuts, chopped
1 tsp. nutmeg
1 tsp. cinnamon
3 oz unsalted butter

How to Prepare:

1. Preheat the oven to 200°-220° Fahrenheit and then coat the pie pan with the unsalted butter and place

the pastry shell inside. Roast the hazelnuts for 10 min. until golden brown.

2. In a saucepan, combine the apples, sugar, apple jam, flour, nutmeg, and cinnamon and boil over low heat with the closed lid for 10 min. Mix in the blueberries and cranberries and cook for 5 min., stirring all the time.

3. Spoon the mixture into the pastry shell and sprinkle the hazelnuts on top, bake for 50-60 min. to serve with the spray cream.

Nutritional Information:

Calories: 195; Total fat: 38 oz; Total carbohydrates: 51 oz; Protein: 20 oz

Berries Apple Pie

Prep Time: 15 min. | _Baking Time: 1 h_ |
Servings: 4

Ingredients:

9" in diameter pie crust (pastry shell)
5 apples, peeled and chopped
half cup of raspberries
half cup of blueberries
half cup of cranberries
1 cup of sugar
5 tbsp. cornstarch
5 tbsp. of blueberry jam
5 tbsp. walnuts
1 tsp. vanilla
3 oz unsalted butter

How to Prepare:

1. Preheat the oven to 200°-220° Fahrenheit and then coat the pie pan with the unsalted butter and place the pastry shell inside. Roast the walnuts for 10 min. until golden brown.
2. In a saucepan, combine the apples, sugar, blueberry jam, cornstarch, and vanilla and boil over low heat with the closed lid for 10 min. Mix in the raspberries, blueberries, and cranberries and cook for 5 min., stirring all the time.
3. Spoon the mixture into the pastry shell and sprinkle the hazelnuts on top, bake for 50-60 min. to serve with the spray cream.

Nutritional Information:

Calories: 195; Total fat: 38 oz; Total carbohydrates: 51 oz; Protein: 20 oz

Honey Apple Pie

Prep Time: 5 min. | Baking Time: 50 min. |
Servings: 4

Ingredients:

2 sour apples, peeled and grated
1 cup of honey
1 cup of wheat flour
5 tbsp. granulated erythritol
3 eggs
1 tsp. baking powder
1 tsp. vanilla
baking spray

How to Prepare:

1. Preheat the oven to 200°-240° Fahrenheit and then coat the silicone pie pan with the baking spray.
2. Beat the eggs with the granulated erythritol using a hand mixer until the mixture becomes foamy and grows in volume at least two times.
3. Add the flour and beat the eggs mixture for 10 min. more. Then mix in the baking powder, vanilla and stir in the honey.
4. Pour the mixture into the silicone pie pan and bake the pie for 50 min. to serve with the spray cream.

Nutritional Information:

Calories: 170; Total fat: 25 oz; Total carbohydrates: 35 oz; Protein: 15 oz

Cream Cheese Apple Pie

Prep Time: 15 min. | ***Baking Time: 1 h*** |
Servings: 4

Ingredients:

9" in diameter pie crust (pastry shell)
5 apples, peeled and sliced
2 eggs
1 cup of cream cheese
1 cup of sugar
half cup of brown sugar
2 tsp. vanilla
2 tsp. cinnamon
3 oz unsalted butter

How to Prepare:

1. Preheat the oven to 200°-220° Fahrenheit and then coat the pie pan with the unsalted butter and place the pastry shell inside.
2. Beat the sugar, cream cheese and vanilla with the eggs using a hand mixer until the foamy mass grows in volume at least two times.
3. Coat the apples with the brown sugar and cinnamon and leave for 10 min.
4. Spoon the cream cheese mixture into the pastry shell and place the sliced apples on top.
5. Sprinkle the cinnamon on top and bake for 50 min. to serve with the spray cream.

Nutritional Information:

Calories: 197; Total fat: 39 oz; Total carbohydrates: 49 oz; Protein: 19 oz

Double Crust Peach Apple Pie

Prep Time: 15 min. | *Baking Time: 50 min.*
Servings: 4

Ingredients:

1 pastry for 9" in diameter double crust apple pie
2 sour apples, peeled and sliced
2 peaches, sliced
2 eggs
1 cup of cream cheese
1 cup of sugar
half cup of brown sugar
2 tsp. vanilla
2 tsp. cinnamon
baking spray

How to Prepare:

1. Preheat the oven to 200°-220° Fahrenheit and then coat the pie pan with the baking spray and place the pastry inside.
2. Beat the sugar, cream cheese and vanilla with the eggs using a hand mixer until the foamy mass grows in volume at least two times.
3. Coat the apples with the brown sugar and cinnamon and leave for 10 min.
4. Spoon the cream cheese mixture into the pastry and place the sliced apples and peaches on top.
5. Cut the second pastry crust into longitudinal stripes to lattice them over the pie and sprinkle the cinnamon on top to bake for 50 min.

Nutritional Information:

Calories: 189; Total fat: 36 oz; Total carbohydrates: 48 oz;
Protein: 21 oz

Walnuts Orange Apple Pie

Prep Time: 10 min. | *Baking Time: 50 min.*
Servings: 4

Ingredients:
9" in diameter pie crust (pastry shell)
5 apples, peeled and chopped
1 orange, sliced
1 cup of sugar
5 tbsp. wheat flour
1 tsp. cinnamon
3 oz unsalted butter

Top Layer Ingredients (Topping):
half cup of sugar
half cup of cornstarch
2 tbsp. orange zest, minced
half cup of oats
5 tbsp. raisins
5 oz unsalted butter
half cup of walnuts

How to Prepare:

1. Preheat the oven to 200°-220° Fahrenheit and then coat the pie pan with the unsalted butter and place the pastry shell inside. Roast the walnuts for 10 min. until light brown.
2. In a bowl, combine the sugar, flour, and cinnamon and stir in the apples, then spoon the mixture into the pastry shell. Place the orange slices on top.
3. Let's get to the topping now – melt the butter over the low heat, stirring all the time and combine all the topping ingredients except for the walnuts until smooth consistency.
4. Spoon the mixture into the pastry shell and bake for 50-60 min.
5. 10 min. before the pie is ready, open the oven and sprinkle the walnuts on top.

Nutritional Information:

Calories: 185; Total fat: 39 oz; Total carbohydrates: 52 oz; Protein: 19 oz

Pecans Lemon Apple Pie

Prep Time: 10 min. | *Baking Time: 50 min.* |
Servings: 4

Ingredients:
9" in diameter pie crust (pastry shell)
5 apples, peeled and chopped
1 lemon, sliced
1 cup of sugar
5 tbsp. wheat flour
1 tsp. cinnamon
baking spray

Top Layer Ingredients (Topping):
half cup of sugar
half cup of cornstarch
2 tbsp. lemon zest, minced
half cup of oats
5 tbsp. raisins
5 oz unsalted butter
half cup of pecans

How to Prepare:

1. Preheat the oven to 200°-220° Fahrenheit and then coat the pie pan with the baking spray and place the pastry shell inside. Roast the pecans for 10 min. until light brown.
2. In a bowl, combine the sugar, flour, and cinnamon and stir in the apples, then spoon the mixture into the pastry shell. Place the lemon slices on top.
3. Let's get to the topping now – melt the butter over the low heat, stirring all the time and combine all the topping ingredients except for the pecans until smooth consistency.

4. Spoon the mixture into the pastry shell and bake for 50-60 min.
5. 10 min. before the pie is ready, open the oven and sprinkle the pecans on top.

Nutritional Information:

Calories: 184; Total fat: 38 oz; Total carbohydrates: 51 oz; Protein: 18 oz

Orange Apple Pie

Prep Time: 10 min. | Baking Time: 55 min. |
Servings: 4

Ingredients:
9" in diameter pie crust (pastry shell)
4 apples, peeled and grated
1 ripe and sweet orange
3 tbsp. orange zest, minced
3 eggs
half cup of cream cheese
1 cup of sugar
1 tsp. baking powder
1 tsp. vanilla
3 oz unsalted butter

How to Prepare:

1. Preheat the oven to 200°-220° Fahrenheit and then coat the pie pan with the unsalted butter and place the pastry shell inside.

2. In a bowl, combine the apples, half of the sugar, baking powder and vanilla and mix well and then spoon the mixture into the pastry shell.
3. Bake the pie for 20 min. and then cool the apple pie, but don't remove from the pie pan.
4. Place the sliced orange on top of the apple pie.
5. Beat the remaining sugar with the cream cheese until the smooth consistency and then add the eggs. Now whisk the cream cheese mixture until smooth consistency.
6. When the mixture is ready spoon it over the apples-oranges pie and bake for 35 min. until the light brown color.

Nutritional Information:

Calories: 201; Total fat: 45 oz; Total carbohydrates: 56 oz; Protein: 26 oz

Cottage Cheese Apple Pie

Prep Time: 15 min. | *Baking Time: 50 min.* |
Servings: 4

Ingredients:

9" in diameter double crust pastry shell
4 sweet apples, peeled and cubed
2 pears, sliced
2 eggs
2 cups of cottage cheese
1 cup of sugar
half cup of brown sugar
2 tsp. vanilla
2 tsp. cinnamon
3 oz unsalted butter

How to Prepare:

1. Preheat the oven to 200°-220° Fahrenheit and then coat the pie pan with the unsalted butter and place the pastry shell inside.
2. Beat the sugar, eggs, and vanilla using a hand mixer until the foamy mass grows in volume at least two times and only then slightly stir in the cottage cheese and mix well.
3. Coat the apples with the brown sugar and cinnamon and leave for 10 min.
4. Combine the cottage cheese mixture with the cubed apples and spoon this mixture into the pastry shell and place the sliced pears on top.
5. Cut the pastry crust into longitudinal stripes to lattice them over the pie and bake for 50 min.

Nutritional Information:

Calories: 234; Total fat: 50 oz; Total carbohydrates: 62 oz; Protein: 39 oz

Summer Apple Pie

Prep Time: 5 min. | **Baking Time: 1 h** | **Servings: 4**

Ingredients:

4 cups of sour Honeycrisp or Melrose apples, cubed
2 cups of Bosc or Anjou pears, cubed
1 cup of wheat flour
1 cup of sugar
4 eggs
1 tsp. baking powder
1 tsp. vanilla
5 oz unsalted butter

How to Prepare:

1. Preheat the oven to 280°-300° Fahrenheit and then coat the pie pan with the butter and leave it in the oven to melt the butter.
2. Beat the eggs with the sugar using a hand mixer until the mixture becomes foamy and grows in volume at least two times.
3. Add the flour and beat the eggs mixture for 10 min. more. Then mix in the baking powder and vanilla.
4. Place the cubed apples and pears into the pie pan and slightly pour the eggs and flour mixture over the fruits.
5. Place the apple-pear pie into the oven and bake it for 1 h to serve with the raspberry jam.

Nutritional Information:

Calories: 169; Total fat: 29 oz; Total carbohydrates: 34 oz; Protein: 17 oz

Exotic Apple Pie

Prep Time: 10 min. | Baking Time: 1 h |
Servings: 4

Ingredients:

2 sweet Cripps Pink apples, cubed
half of the pineapple, cubed
1 banana, cubed
1 kiwi sliced
5 tbsp. shredded coconut
1 cup of almond flour
1 cup of sugar
4 eggs
1 tsp. baking powder
1 tsp. vanilla
5 oz unsalted butter

How to Prepare:

1. Preheat the oven to 280°-300° Fahrenheit and then coat the pie pan with the butter and leave it in the oven to melt the butter.

2. Beat the eggs with the sugar using a hand mixer until the mixture becomes foamy and grows in volume at least two times.
3. Add the almond flour and beat the eggs mixture for 10 min. more. Then mix in the baking powder and vanilla.
4. Place the cubed apples, pineapple and banana into the pie pan and slightly pour the eggs and almond flour mixture over the fruits.
5. Place the apple pie into the oven and bake it for 1 h and then 10 min. before the pie is ready, open the oven and place kiwi slices on top.

Nutritional Information:

Calories: 168; Total fat: 30 oz; Total carbohydrates: 39 oz; Protein: 18 oz

Mango Apple Pie

Prep Time: 10 min. | Baking Time: 55 min. |
Servings: 4

Ingredients:

9" in diameter pie crust (pastry shell)
4 apples, peeled and grated
1 big mango, peeled and sliced
3 eggs
half cup of cream cheese
1 cup of sugar
1 tsp. baking powder
1 tsp. cinnamon
3 oz unsalted butter

How to Prepare:

1. Preheat the oven to 200°-220° Fahrenheit and then coat the pie pan with the unsalted butter and place the pastry shell inside.
2. In a bowl, combine the apples, half of the sugar, baking powder and vanilla and mix well and then spoon the mixture into the pastry shell.
3. Place the sliced mango on top of the apple pie.
4. Beat the remaining sugar with the cream cheese until the smooth consistency and then add the eggs. Now whisk the cream cheese mixture until smooth consistency.
5. When the mixture is ready spoon it over the apples-mango pie and bake for 55 min. until the light brown color.

Nutritional Information:

Calories: 199; Total fat: 47 oz; Total carbohydrates: 57 oz; Protein: 25 oz

Traditional Apple Charlotte

Prep Time: 5 min. | **Baking Time: 1 h** | **Servings: 4**

Ingredients:

4 cups of sour and crisp Granny Smith apples, cubed
1 cup of wheat flour
1 cup of sugar
4 eggs
2 tsp. baking soda
baking spray

How to Prepare:

1. Preheat the oven to 280°-300° Fahrenheit and then coat the silicone pie pan with the baking spray.
2. Beat the eggs with the sugar using a hand mixer until the mixture becomes foamy and grows in volume at least two times.
3. Add the flour and beat the eggs mixture for 10 min. more. Then mix in the baking soda.
4. Place the cubed apples into the pie pan and slightly pour the eggs and flour mixture over the apples.
5. Place the apple pie into the oven and bake it for 1 h to serve with the strawberry jam and cream cheese.

Nutritional Information:

Calories: 171; Total fat: 30 oz; Total carbohydrates: 35 oz; Protein: 18 oz

Pear Apple Layer Torte

Prep Time: 15 min. | *Baking Time: 1 h* |
Servings: 4

Ingredients:

4 sour apples, grated
4 pears, grated
1 cup of wheat flour
1 cup of semolina
1 cup of brown sugar
2 tsp. baking powder
2 tbsp. cinnamon
2 tbsp. vanilla
5 oz unsalted butter, sliced
baking spray

How to Prepare:

1. Preheat the oven to 280°-300° Fahrenheit and then coat the pie pan with the baking spray.
2. Sprinkle the grated apples with the cinnamon and leave for 10 min. and the gated pears with the vanilla.
3. In a big kitchen bowl, combine the wheat flour, semolina, baking powder, and brown sugar and mix well.
4. Spoon 1/3 of the mixture into the pie pan and flatten with the spoon. Then place the grated apples and flatten with the spoon. After that, place the flour mixture on top and cover it with the grated pears. Make one apple, one pear and three flour layers, remember that the flour mixture should be on top.
5. Place the sliced butter on top to cover the torte surface completely and bake the apple torte for 1 h.

Nutritional Information:

Calories: 179; Total fat: 36 oz; Total carbohydrates: 41 oz; Protein: 23 oz

Russian Choco Apple Sharlotka

Prep Time: 5 min. | Baking Time: 1 h | Servings: 4

Ingredients:

5 apples, cubed
1 cup of wheat flour
1 cup of brown sugar
half cup of cocoa powder
3 eggs
4 tbsp. butter, cubed
2 tsp. baking powder
1 tsp. vanilla
baking spray

How to Prepare:

1. Preheat the oven to 280°-300° Fahrenheit and then coat the pie pan with the baking spray.

2. Beat the eggs with the sugar using a hand mixer until the mixture becomes foamy and grows in volume at least two times.
3. Add the flour and cocoa powder and beat the eggs mixture for 10 min. more. Then mix in the baking powder.
4. Place the cubed apples and butter into the pie pan and slightly pour the eggs and flour mixture over the apples.
5. Place the apple pie into the oven and bake it for 1 h to serve with the cream spray.

Nutritional Information:

Calories: 172; Total fat: 32 oz; Total carbohydrates: 37 oz; Protein: 19 oz

Chocolate Apple Charlotte

Prep Time: 5 min. | Baking Time: 1 h | Servings: 4

Ingredients:

5 apples, cubed
1 cup of wheat flour
1 cup of brown sugar
half cup of cocoa powder
1 cup of dark chocolate, cubed
3 eggs
2 tsp. baking soda
1 tsp. vanilla
baking spray

How to Prepare:

1. Preheat the oven to 280°-300° Fahrenheit and then coat the pie pan with the baking spray.
2. Beat the eggs with the sugar using a hand mixer until the mixture becomes foamy and grows in volume at least two times.
3. Add the flour and cocoa powder and beat the eggs mixture for 10 min. more. Then mix in the baking soda.
4. Place the cubed apples into the pie pan and slightly pour the eggs and flour mixture over the apples.
5. Place the apple pie into the oven and bake it for 1 h. Melt the dark chocolate in a double boiler for 20 minutes, stirring all the time. Pour the melted dark chocolate over the cake and place in the fridge for around 30 min.

Nutritional Information:

Calories: 180; Total fat: 33 oz; Total carbohydrates: 40 oz; Protein: 23 oz

Cinnamon Apple Charlotte

Prep Time: 10 min. | *Baking Time: 50 min.* | *Servings: 4*

Ingredients:

5 sour apples, cubed
3 tbsp. cinnamon, grated
2 tbsp. cinnamon extract
1 cup of wheat flour
1 cup of sugar
3 eggs
2 tsp. baking soda
3 oz unsalted butter

How to Prepare:

1. Preheat the oven to 300°-320° Fahrenheit and then coat the pie pan with the butter.
2. In a bowl, combine the cubed apples with the ground cinnamon.
3. Beat the eggs with the sugar using a hand mixer until the mixture becomes foamy and grows in volume at least two times.
4. Add the flour and cinnamon extract and beat the eggs mixture for 10 min. more. Then mix in the baking soda.
5. Place the cubed apples into the pie pan and slightly pour the eggs and flour mixture over the apples and bake for around 50 min. until golden brown and crispy.

Nutritional Information:

Calories: 176; Total fat: 31 oz; Total carbohydrates: 37 oz; Protein: 20 oz

Lemon Apple Charlotte

Prep Time: 10 min. | Baking Time: 55 min. | Servings: 4

Ingredients:

5 apples, sliced
5 tbsp. unsalted butter
1 cup of wheat flour
2 tbsp. lemon zest, minced
half cup of lemon juice
2 tbsp. cinnamon
1 cup of sugar
3 eggs
2 tsp. baking soda
baking spray

How to Prepare:

1. Preheat the oven to 280°-310° Fahrenheit and then coat the pie pan with the baking spray.

2. In a saucepan, melt the butter and add the sliced apples, minced lemon zest, lemon juice, and cinnamon and cook for around 10-15 min.
3. Beat the eggs with the sugar using a hand mixer until the mixture becomes foamy and grows in volume at least two times.
4. Add the flour and beat the eggs mixture for 10 min. more. Then mix in the baking soda and pour the mixture into the apples and mix well.
5. Spoon the apple mixture into the pie pan and bake for 55 min. until golden brown and crispy.

Nutritional Information:

Calories: 181; Total fat: 32 oz; Total carbohydrates: 39 oz; Protein: 21 oz

Nuts Apple Charlotte

Prep Time: 10 min. | *Baking Time: 55 min.* | *Servings: 4*

Ingredients:

5 apples, cubed
half cup of walnuts, ground
half cup of peanuts, ground
5 tbsp. unsalted butter
5 tbsp. cream cheese
1 cup of wheat flour
2 tbsp. vanilla
1 cup of sugar
3 eggs
2 tsp. baking powder
baking spray

How to Prepare:

1. Preheat the oven to 280°-310° Fahrenheit and then coat the pie pan with the baking spray and roast the walnuts with peanuts for 10 min. until crispy.
2. In a saucepan, melt the butter and add the cubed apples, cream cheese, and vanilla and cook for 10 min.
3. Beat the eggs with the sugar using a hand mixer until the mixture becomes foamy and grows in volume at least two times.
4. Add the flour and beat the eggs mixture for 10 min. more. Then mix in the baking soda and nuts and spoon the mixture into the apples and mix well.
5. Spoon the apple mixture into the pie pan and bake for 1 h until golden brown and crispy.

Nutritional Information:

Calories: 182; Total fat: 33 oz; Total carbohydrates: 42 oz; Protein: 23 oz

Orange Almond Apple Charlotte

Prep Time: 10 min. | Baking Time: 55 min. | Servings: 4

Ingredients:
5 apples, cubed
2 tbsp. orange zest, minced
half cup of orange juice
2 tbsp. almond extract
5 tbsp. unsalted butter
1 cup of wheat flour
2 tbsp. vanilla
1 cup of sugar
2 eggs
2 tsp. baking powder
baking spray

How to Prepare:

1. Preheat the oven to 280°-310° Fahrenheit and then coat the pie pan with the baking spray.
2. In a saucepan, melt the butter and add the cubed apples, orange zest, orange juice, almond extract, and vanilla and cook for 10 min.
3. Beat the eggs with the sugar using a hand mixer until the mixture becomes foamy and grows in volume at least two times.
4. Add the flour and beat the eggs mixture for 10 min. more. Then mix in the baking powder and spoon the mixture into the apples and mix well.
5. Spoon the apple mixture into the pie pan and bake for 55 min. until golden brown and crispy.

Nutritional Information:

Calories: 183; Total fat: 34 oz; Total carbohydrates: 43 oz; Protein: 24 oz

Standard Apple Pie

Prep Time: 15 min. | *Baking Time: 55 min.* |
Servings: 4

Ingredients:

1 pastry for 9" in diameter double crust apple pie
3 sour apples, peeled and grated
3 sweet apples, peeled and grated
3 tbsp. lime juice
5 tbsp. wheat flour
half cup of sugar
half tsp. nutmeg
2 tsp. cinnamon
3 oz unsalted butter, sliced
baking spray

How to Prepare:

1. Preheat the oven to 200°-220° Fahrenheit and then coat the pie pan with the baking spray and press the pastry inside the pie pan.
2. Combine the grated apples, sugar, flour, nutmeg, cinnamon, and lime juice and spoon into the pie pan.
3. Coat the apples with the second part of the crust and pinch the sides of both crust parts carefully.
4. Place the sliced butter on top and bake for 20 min. on high heat and then on medium heat for another 25 min.

Nutritional Information:

Calories: 179; Total fat: 37 oz; Total carbohydrates: 49 oz; Protein: 20 oz

Standard Nuts Apple Pie

Prep Time: 15 min. | Baking Time: 50 min. |
Servings: 4

Ingredients:

1 pastry for 9" in diameter double crust apple pie
5 apples, peeled and grated
half cup hazelnuts, ground
half cup walnut halves
half cup peanuts, ground
2 tbsp. lemon juice
3 tbsp. wheat flour
half cup of sugar
2 tsp. cinnamon
3 oz unsalted butter, sliced
baking spray

How to Prepare:

1. Preheat the oven to 250°-280° Fahrenheit and then coat the pie pan with the baking spray and press the pastry inside the pie pan.
2. Combine the grated apples, sugar, flour, cinnamon, lemon juice, hazelnuts and peanuts, and spoon into the pie pan.
3. Coat the apples with the second part of the crust and pinch the sides of both crust parts carefully.
4. Place the sliced butter and walnut halves on top and bake for 50 min. until golden brown.

Nutritional Information:

Calories: 174; Total fat: 33 oz; Total carbohydrates: 46 oz; Protein: 19 oz

Cream Cheese Walnuts Apple Pie

Ingredients:

1 pastry for 9" in diameter double crust apple pie
5 apples, peeled and grated
half cup walnuts, ground
1 cup cream cheese
3 tbsp. wheat flour
1 cup of sugar
2 tsp. vanilla
3 oz unsalted butter, sliced
baking spray

How to Prepare:

1. Preheat the oven to 250°-280° Fahrenheit and then coat the pie pan with the baking spray and press the pastry inside the pie pan.
2. Combine the grated apples, wheat flour, vanilla, and walnuts.
3. Beat the cream cheese with the sugar using a hand mixer until the smooth and creamy consistency.
4. Slightly combine the apple mixture with the cream cheese mixture and mix well.
5. Coat the apples with the second part of the crust and pinch the sides of both crust parts carefully.
6. Use a knife or a spoon to make the slits in the top crust layer and place the sliced butter on top.
7. Bake the apple pie for 1 hour until the top of the pie is golden and crispy. Serve with the ice cream.

Nutritional Information:

Calories: 175; Total fat: 35 oz; Total carbohydrates: 44 oz; Protein: 21 oz

Orange Apple Torte

Prep Time: 15 min. | *Baking Time: 1 h 30 min.* |
Servings: 4

Ingredients:

4 sour apples, grated
4 oranges, sliced
1 tbsp. orange zest, minced
1 cup of wheat flour
1 cup of semolina
1 cup of sugar
2 tsp. baking powder
2 tbsp. cinnamon
5 oz unsalted butter, sliced
baking spray

How to Prepare:

1. Preheat the oven to 280°-300° Fahrenheit and then coat the pie pan with the baking spray.
2. Sprinkle the grated apples with the cinnamon and leave for 10 min.
3. In a big kitchen bowl, combine the wheat flour, semolina, baking powder, sugar and orange zest.
4. Spoon 1/3 of the mixture into the pie pan and flatten with the spoon. Then place the grated apples and half of the oranges on top. After that place the flour mixture on top and cover it with the sliced oranges to top with the flour mixture. Make one apple, two oranges and three flour layers, remember that the flour mixture goes on top.
5. Place the sliced butter on top to cover the torte surface completely and bake the apple torte for 1.5 h.

Nutritional Information:

Calories: 180; Total fat: 38 oz; Total carbohydrates: 42 oz;
Protein: 24 oz

Kiwi Apple Torte

Prep Time: 15 min. | Baking Time: 1 h 30 min. |
Servings: 4

Ingredients:
4 sour apples, grated
6 kiwis, peeled and sliced
1 cup of wheat flour
1 cup of semolina
1 cup of sugar
2 tsp. baking powder
2 tbsp. cinnamon
5 oz unsalted butter, sliced
baking spray

How to Prepare:

1. Preheat the oven to 280°-300° Fahrenheit and then coat the pie pan with the baking spray.

2. Sprinkle the grated apples with the cinnamon and leave for 10 min.
3. In a big kitchen bowl, combine the wheat flour, semolina, baking powder, and sugar.
4. Spoon 1/3 of the mixture into the pie pan and flatten with the spoon. Then spoon the grated apples and place half of the kiwis on top. After that place the flour mixture on top and cover it with the sliced kiwis and then top with the flour mixture. Make one apple, two kiwis and three flour layers, remember that the flour mixture goes on top.
5. Place the sliced butter on top to cover the torte surface completely and bake the apple torte for 1.5 h to serve with the vanilla-strawberry ice cream.

Nutritional Information:
Calories: 182; Total fat: 39 oz; Total carbohydrates: 46 oz; Protein: 25 oz

Chocolate Apple Cake

Prep Time: 10 min. | Baking Time: 55 min. | Servings: 6

Ingredients:

5 sweet apples, peeled and grated
1 package of Dark chocolate cake mix
1 cup dark chocolate
1 cup of caramel sauce
4 oz unsalted butter, sliced
2 tsp. vanilla
baking spray

How to Prepare:

1. Preheat the oven to 230°-250° Fahrenheit and then coat the pie pan with the baking spray.
2. Follow the instructions suggested on the packet to prepare the Dark chocolate cake mix and combine the mix with the apples, butter, and vanilla. Then stir in the caramel sauce and mix well until the homogenous mass.
3. Bake the apple cake for 1 hour and then melt the dark chocolate on low heat for around 10 min., stirring all the time and after cooling pour it slowly over the apple pie to serve!

Nutritional Information:

Calories: 153; Total fat: 26 oz; Total carbohydrates: 33 oz; Protein: 15 oz

Red Velvet Apple Cake

Prep Time: 5 min. | **Baking Time: 1 h** | **Servings: 6**

Ingredients:

1 package of Red velvet cake mix
5 sour apples, peeled and grated
5 tbsp. strawberry jam
5 tbsp. raspberry jam
half cup of brown sugar
5 oz unsalted butter, sliced
2 tsp. vanilla

How to Prepare:

1. Preheat the oven to 150°-180° Fahrenheit and then coat the pie pan with the butter and leave it in the oven to melt the butter.
2. Follow the instructions suggested on the packet to prepare the Red velvet mix and combine the mix with the apples, strawberry jam, raspberry jam sugar, and vanilla.
3. Bake the cake for around 1 hour and then cool the red velvet apple cake and place it into the fridge for at least a few hours to serve with the strawberry spray cream and cappuccino.

Nutritional Information:

Calories: 140; Total fat: 24 oz; Total carbohydrates: 29 oz; Protein: 14 oz

Plum Apple Torte

Prep Time: 15 min. | Baking Time: 1 h 30 min. |
Servings: 4

Ingredients:

2 sour apples, grated
2 sweet apples, grated
2 cups of plums, cubed
1 cup of plum jam
1 cup of wheat flour
1 cup of semolina
1 cup of sugar
2 tsp. baking soda
2 tbsp. cinnamon
5 oz unsalted butter, sliced
baking spray

How to Prepare:

1. Preheat the oven to 280°-300° Fahrenheit and then coat the pie pan with the baking spray.

2. Sprinkle the grated apples with the cinnamon and leave for 10 min.
3. In a big kitchen bowl, combine the wheat flour, semolina, baking soda, and sugar.
4. Spoon 1/3 of the mixture into the pie pan and flatten with the spoon. Then spoon the grated apples and half of the plum jam on top. After that, place the flour mixture on top and cover it with the cubed plums and then top with the flour mixture. Make one apple and plum jam, one cubed plums, and three flour layers, remember that the flour mixture goes on top.
5. Place the sliced butter on top to cover the torte surface completely and bake the apple torte for 1.5 h. Cool the apple torte and spoon the rest of the plum jam on top. Serve the plum apple torte with the cream cheese and cocoa.

Nutritional Information:

Calories: 184; Total fat: 39 oz; Total carbohydrates: 44 oz; Protein: 22 oz

Conclusion

Thank you for buying this apple pie cookbook. I hope this cookbook was able to help you to prepare delicious apple dessert recipes.

If you've enjoyed this book, I'd greatly appreciate if you could leave an honest review on Amazon.

Reviews are very important to us authors, and it only takes a minute for you to post.

Your direct feedback could be used to help other readers to discover the advantages of apple pie recipes!

Thank you again and I hope you have enjoyed this cookbook.

Made in the USA
Middletown, DE
13 December 2021